For my grandchildren: Zoe, Eleni, Vasili, and Emanuel~MR

For my husband, Régis Felix Galand~IB

Saint Anthony the Great
Text © 2015 John Chryssavgis & Marilyn Rouvelas
Illustrations © 2015 Isabelle Brent

Wisdom Tales is an imprint of World Wisdom, Inc.

Library of Congress Cataloging-in-Publication Data

Chryssavgis, John, author.
Saint Anthony the Great / by John Chryssavgis & Marilyn Rouvelas ;
Illustrated by Isabelle Brent.
pages cm
ISBN 978-1-937786-46-5
1. Anthony, of Egypt, Saint, approximately 250-355 or 356--Juvenile literature.
2. Christian saints--Juvenile literature. I. Rouvelas, Marilyn, author.
II. Brent, Isabelle, illustrator. III. Title.
BR1720.A6C479 2015
270.1092--dc23
[B]
2015023673

Printed in China on acid-free paper.
Production Date: July 2015,
Plant & Location: Printed by 1010 Printing International Ltd,
Job/Batch #: TT15060899

For information address Wisdom Tales, P.O. Box 2682,
Bloomington, Indiana 47402-2682
www.wisdomtalespress.com

SAINT ANTHONY THE GREAT

By

John Chryssavgis & Marilyn Rouvelas

Illustrated by Isabelle Brent

✣ Wisdom Tales ✣

Many years ago in Egypt, a young man named Anthony began a long trip to a place close by.

Anthony was born in Koma, Egypt. His parents were Christian. He was a happy child. When he was about nineteen years old, Anthony's parents died, leaving him and his sister alone. His heart was sad. What should he do? At church one day, Anthony heard Christ's advice in the Bible. "If you want to be perfect, go, sell all you own. Give to the poor. Then you will have treasure in heaven. Come, follow me" (Matthew 19:21).

All at once Anthony sold everything he owned. The money went to someone to take care of his sister and poor people. Anthony set out with nothing to find something.

His parents were not there to answer his questions. So Anthony asked some wise old men. How could his heart be changed? The wise men were kind and patient. They prayed. They loved everyone. Maybe Anthony could copy them and help his heart.

But the devil tried to stop Anthony. He made a dust cloud of wrong thoughts in Anthony's mind. Anthony began to think he was better than his friends. His head filled with mean things to say to people who made him angry. Jealous thoughts and wanting other people's things made even more dust.

Anthony fought these thoughts by calling on God to help. The dust cloud went away, and his heart felt better. The devil had lost his first fight with Anthony.

Anthony still did not have all the answers about his heart. He decided to go into the desert. Only a few people lived there. Maybe he would learn something if he was quiet, still, and alone.

He chose as his new home an empty cave near his village. His friends brought him food and water for thirteen years. The devil and his helpers sometimes visited. Anthony fought them again with prayers. He said a Psalm to himself. "If an army should rise up against me, my heart will not be afraid" (27:3).

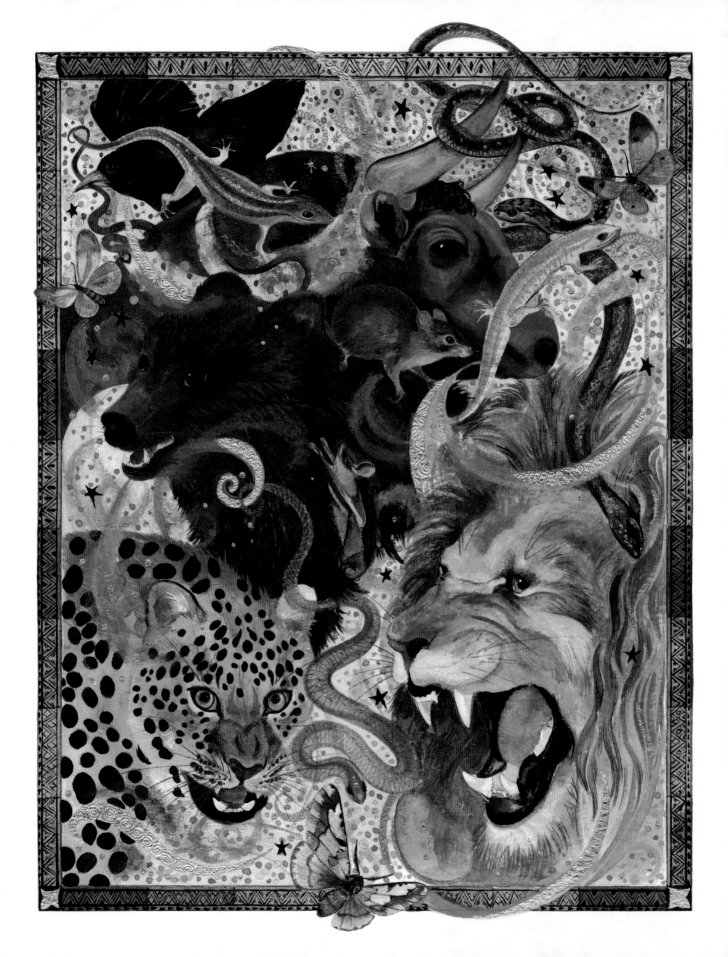

One night the demons seemed to come through the walls.
They looked like lions, bears, leopards, bulls, snakes, and
wolves. They didn't attack Anthony. Something was holding
them back. The roof opened. A bright stream of light shone on
Anthony. Scared, the enemies left the cave.

Anthony knew that the light was from God. God had saved
him. Later Anthony told his friends, "I'm no longer afraid of
anything, because I love God."

Anthony left the cave the next day. He went farther into the desert to Mount Pispir. But the devil still wanted him to do wrong things and tempted him. He put a make-believe silver dish on the road. Would Anthony steal it? Anthony shouted "No!" to the devil. The silver dish went up in smoke. Then a mound of real gold appeared. Did Anthony want to have it? Again Anthony said "No!" He wanted to say "Yes!" only to God.

Anthony then found an old fort where he could live alone. Friends sent down food and water to him from the rooftop. One time they looked through a hole in the wall and saw demons. Anthony shouted for his friends to make the sign of the cross to be safe.

Anthony learned that these creatures were not always real. They were his thoughts that were out of control. Sometimes he got very angry. Sometimes he got very jealous. Sometimes he didn't want to share. These wrong thoughts kept him from being close to God. Right thoughts like being patient and caring for his friends, brought him nearer to God.

After twenty years his friends tore down the door of the fort. They saw that Anthony was healthy and his heart was pure.

Anthony's pure heart loved others, loved itself, loved the world, and loved God.

God had been in Anthony's heart all along. God did good things through him. He healed a young woman so she could walk. He helped a blind man to see. He made sad hearts glad. His happy face reflected his joyful heart. The Bible says, "A glad heart makes the face glow" (Proverbs 15:13).

People moved to the desert to live near Anthony. Little huts and tents spread through the hills. People were singing, praying, and helping each other. Anthony taught them, "If you love your neighbor, you love God. If you love God, you also love your own soul."

Anthony had become a wise old man. People would ask him about how to lead a good life. He told them that having wrong thoughts was natural. Fighting them made the heart stronger. Wrong thoughts could be replaced by right thoughts of peace, courage, joy, and love of God and others.

God was doing many miracles through Anthony. People praised him all the time. But Anthony did not want to become proud and think he was better than others. He left again.

He went farther into the desert to Mount Colzim. At the bottom of the mountain there was a spring of cool water and space for a garden and visitors. Up the mountain was a cave where he could be quiet, still, and alone. These two places were just right. Sometimes he could be by himself, and sometimes with others.

He lived forty-three years there with almost nothing. A visitor once asked how he could live without books. Anthony answered, "My book is nature. It is always nearby when I wish to read the words of God."

To protect his heart from wrong thoughts, he would keep busy by weaving palm leaves into baskets. Friends took them to be sold so he could buy food.

The Life of Anthony

Anthony left the cave the next day. He went farther into the desert to Mount Pispir.

But the devil still wanted him to do wrong things and tempted him.

Anthony died in the cave at 105 years old. His friend, Archbishop Athanasius, wrote a book about his life. He described Anthony as being patient, humble, loving, and calm. He had a pure soul and a glad heart.

Anthony had learned that the journey he started when he was young was short. It was a trip inside himself to discover God. This led thousands of people to become like Anthony and also find God in their hearts.

Appendix
The Life of Saint Anthony

Sometime in the last years of his life, Athanasius, Archbishop of Alexandria (c. 296–373), wrote *The Life of Anthony*, sketching the classic portrait of his close friend and advisor, Anthony of Egypt (c. 251–356). Anthony implored his disciples not to reveal his gravesite to anyone. He left behind only some clothing to his closest followers as well as "a sheepskin and an old cloak" for Athanasius.

His biographer, however, left behind a legacy far greater than any monument, bequeathing to later centuries the memoir of an extraordinary pioneer and mystic who influenced such great thinkers as Basil of Caesarea and Gregory of Nyssa, Augustine of Hippo and Benedict of Nursia, Thomas Aquinas and, more recently, Thomas Merton. Despite his hardship and struggle in the desert, Anthony's lessons on monasticism as the way of the Gospel, on the importance of silence and fasting, and on the practice of charity and love, proved both endearing and enduring.

Apart from the Bible, perhaps no other book has had more immense influence on Christian monastic and religious life than *The Life of Anthony*. Although Anthony's initial actions and move into the desert were little noticed outside his village, by the time of his death, he had become known as "the father of monasticism," and the surrounding "desert had become a city." He was one of the first of many Christian Desert Fathers, who lived primarily in the Egyptian desert during the third and fourth centuries and are remembered for their wisdom through pithy sayings.

In the same way that *The Life of Anthony* has captivated countless men and women of all ages through the centuries, this retelling can capture the attention of young readers and encourage their interest in such timeless spiritual qualities as the importance of stillness in an ever-changing world, the value of prayer in an ever-troubled world, and the power of compassion in a world filled with selfish competition and violent conflict. Anthony's battle with his demons, as well as his struggle to acquire sensitivity toward others and a pure heart for God, can prove to be compelling lessons leading to a life of love and prayer. This is a timeless story about the victory of good over evil inside us and around us.

Timeline*

c. 251	Anthony is born in Koma, Egypt
269	Anthony's parents die
270	Anthony sells his possessions
270–271	Anthony lives alone and seeks advice from wise elders
272–285	Anthony lives alone in an abandoned cave/tomb for thirteen years
285–305	Anthony lives alone in an abandoned fort at Mount Pispir for twenty years
306–313	Anthony lives in a community for seven years
313–356	Anthony lives alone in a cave at Mount Colzim for forty-three years
356	Anthony dies at the age of 105
360	Athanasius writes *The Life of Anthony*

*Dates are approximate

Further Reading

Athanasius, The Life of Anthony. The Coptic Life and the Greek Life. Translated by Tim Vivian and Apostolos N. Athanassakis. Kalamazoo, MI: Cistercian Publications, 2003.

The Desert Fathers. Translated by Helen Waddell. New York: Vintage Spiritual Classics, 1998.

In the Heart of the Desert, Revised: The Spirituality of the Desert Fathers and Mothers. By John Chryssavgis. Bloomington, IN: World Wisdom, 2008.

The Letters of Saint Anthony the Great. Translated by Derwas J. Chitty. Fairacres, Oxford: SLG Press Convent of the Incarnation, 1975.

The Sayings of the Desert Fathers: The Alphabetical Collection. Translated by Benedicta Ward. Kalamazoo, MI: Cistercian Publications, 1975.

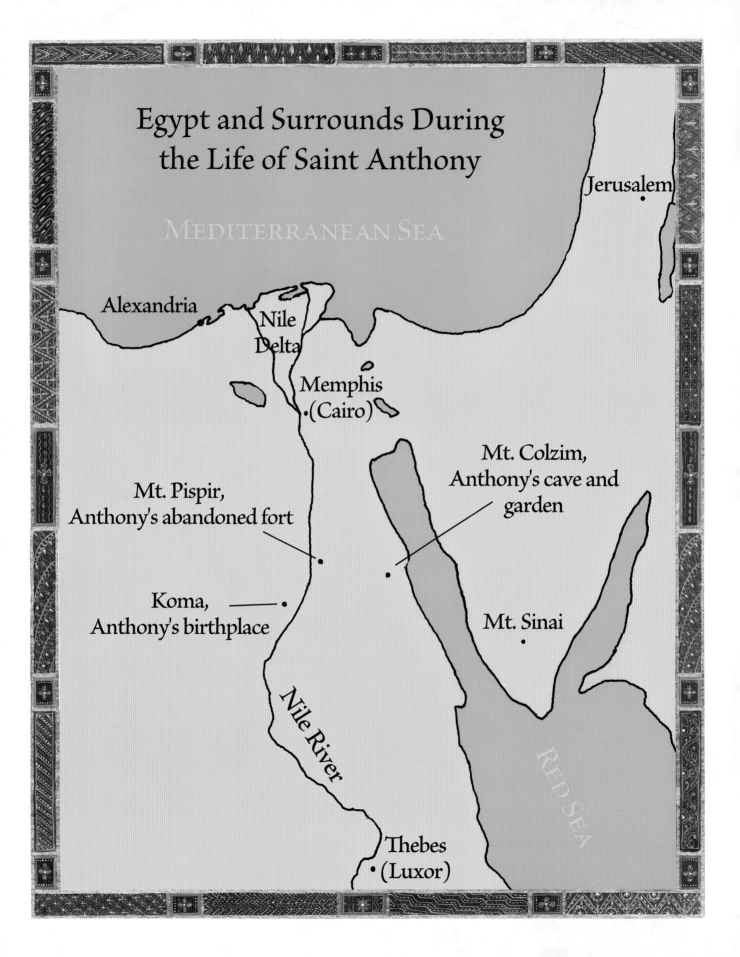

Egypt and Surrounds During
the Life of Saint Anthony

MEDITERRANEAN SEA

Jerusalem

Alexandria

Nile
Delta

Memphis
(Cairo)

Mt. Colzim,
Anthony's cave and
garden

Mt. Pispir,
Anthony's abandoned fort

Koma,
Anthony's birthplace

Mt. Sinai

Nile River

RED SEA

Thebes
(Luxor)

Glossary

Devil / Demons: Facing and fighting the demons means coming to terms with oneself and becoming an integrated human being. It involves recognizing one's wrong conduct and passions, deeper motivations, and personal weaknesses; assuming responsibility; and making right choices. The struggle can sometimes be fierce and raw.

Desert: More than simply a geographical location, the desert is symbolical of the place where one cannot hide from God and from oneself. It is the place where one struggles and battles with one's deepest desires and temptations. It can be a time or place of quiet or aloneness, a space of reflection or transformation.

Heart: Besides being the physical organ, the heart signifies the spiritual center of the human being, the entire person attuned to God. The heart is the place where heaven and earth meet. In the spiritual life, entering one's heart leads to acquiring sacred knowledge of fundamental truths.

Old Man: The *geron* (in Greek), *abba* (in Coptic), *staretz* (in Russian), and *pater* (in Latin) all mean a guide and companion in the spiritual journey. The importance of a spiritual elder, male or female (the terms for female monastic guides are *amma* or *mater*), has been underlined since the emergence of Christian monasticism and especially in the life of Saint Anthony, who consulted elders and subsequently became an elder himself. The implication is that one is never healed alone. The core of the wisdom of the desert is found in the sayings of these spiritual elders.

Quiet / Stillness: The spiritual path leading to stillness and inner tranquility. It is the method of learning to listen and to be open to God. Learning to live with one's self ultimately leads to learning to love others.

Thoughts: In the "sayings" of the early Desert Fathers and Mothers, the battle between good and evil takes place on the level of thoughts (or temptations) in the mind and heart. Often provoked or suggested by demons, such disturbances are natural, but not considered sinful unless one consents or concedes to them. Moreover, evil thoughts can be transformed into good thoughts by divine grace through prayer, watchfulness, and constant struggle.